Help for

WOMEN

with

ADHD

My Simple Strategies for
Conquering Chaos

JOAN WILDER

Copyright © 2016 by Joan Wilder

This book is not intended as a substitute for the medical advice of physicians. Any information on health care or health-related topics is not medical advice and should not be treated as such. The reader should regularly consult a physician in matters relating to his/her health and particularly with respect to the use of medications or any symptoms that may require diagnosis or medical attention.

Kindle edition by:

Joan Wilder
Boston, MA
joan.wilder@gmail.com

CONTENTS

WHAT IT'S LIKE

I wake up and it starts: The ideas, the choices, the impulses to go in 10 directions at once.

The only thing I'm sure I'll do is have coffee. After that, it's anybody's guess.

I don't work a 9 to 5 job so I don't have a routine, which is both good and bad for someone like me. The good part is the freedom I have to do what I want. The bad part is that a free schedule leaves me vulnerable to a mind that can get swamped with options, excited about lots of possibilities, and ends up so overwhelmed, I do nothing.

Sometimes coffee launches me into a pretty good day. But if I'm off my game, I'll be anxious even during coffee, guilty that I'm not doing this, or that, and thinking that I should be …

I should be …

I should be …

I should be meditating, it might occur to me, because I know it's so helpful. But, on a bad day, I won't want to stick with the type of meditation I've been using (sort of) for a while, and think that another method would be better. Before you know it, I'm exploring guided meditation apps on my phone – and once I go that route, I'm off and running.

Yes! Of course! I need to run, I'll think, suddenly remembering that I've already decided that if I don't go to the gym first thing, I won't go. So, forget the meditation: I've promised myself I'd go to the gym this morning, and I just can't let myself down. Again.

Oh, but God, the kitchen's a mess. And, I've got to get my clothes together so I'll have something good to wear to a work meeting late this afternoon. Oh, and I have to print the documents I need to take with me (is there enough ink in the cartridge?) And,

I have to make those two doctor's appointments and postpone that other one. And, I want to research laser printers, these ink jets are junk. And, I have to drop by my friend's new restaurant: I should take her something. Then the floodgates completely open with thoughts I can't scribble fast enough to get down: write my editor back by noon at the latest (What did I decide to tell her? Where are my notes?), call my Aunt Chris, start writing that article – when's it due? Figure out something for dinner, get a card for my niece, a birthday gift for my sister …

Stop. STOP. Breathe.

Okay, I decide. I'll just go to the gym. That will get things rolling in the right direction. Gym day is always a good day.

Before putting my sweats on, I can't help but grab the new top I just got in the mail and try it on. It really is too small. Shoot. I rip it off and, naked, without thinking, I grab my beading set-up from the shelf and string two little beads on the necklace I have half started before forcing myself to put it down.

In the couple minutes it takes to get dressed, I'm making a fabulous, lawyer-like case to myself about just taking a walk in the neighborhood, rather than going to the gym. Actually, says this voice in my head, you should really just get a used treadmill – that would be easier: There must be tons of them on Craigslist, I think, as I grab my computer …

No! No, no, no!

* * *

Are you with me? If you often feel overwhelmed, impulsive, foggy-headed, or disorganized, you're not alone. Between 4 and 8 percent of American adults have ADHD (Attention Deficit Hyperactivity Disorder/Attention Deficit Disorder/ADD), and experts estimate that thousands more are undiagnosed.

Everybody experiences everything ADHDers experience, but to a lesser extent. So, even if you haven't been formally diagnosed, you may be dealing with attention deficit symptoms as a result of a number of stressors (post-partum hormones, PMS, menopause, dietary sensitivities). And, if that's the case, this book can help you, too.

The core irregularity that generates the most distressing behavior is a difficulty controlling the way you pay attention and focus on things. This makes it an effort to plan, organize, and generally regulate and manage your time, money, obligations, or belongings, despite the fact that ADHDers are often very bright, intuitive, creative, and inventive. These issues play out in a number of behaviors like confusion when trying to get things done, forgetfulness, an inability to prioritize needs and desires, and failure to follow through doing what you most want to do.

I sometimes think that having ADHD is like being a fantastic orchestra – with a full house of great players – and a slightly off conductor!

Along with irregular focus, is a mind that's hyper-aware of a tremendous volume of information from the environment and an often-urgent sense that something needs to be done, or said, about everything. The mind is continually hatching impassioned ideas and thoughts, in response to its surroundings. The new ideas feel so important that whatever it was you were doing, before they popped into your head, drops off your radar. This feeling of urgency is linked with impulsivity, another hallmark of ADHD.

This short book focuses on these challenges and corresponding tools you can use to maneuver around and through them. And, although it was written for women with ADHD, the tools will work even if your challenges are less severe, or temporary.

Some of the most common, and troublesome, issues are:

Difficulty prioritizing;

Getting distracted by ideas and sensations that disrupt your concentration;

Difficulty following through on what you were so excited about yesterday;

Misplacing important items you use daily, like your phone, keys, or wallet;

Running late, losing track of time, or not having time to finish tasks properly;

Difficulty deciding and choosing;

Feeling overwhelmed by complex or backlogged tasks, or by overly stimulating environments;

Impulsive ideas or actions that lead you away from your intended goals;

Procrastination on necessary tasks or big projects;

Changing your mind all the time.

Does one item on this list scream your name? Maybe all of them do. If you want, you can fly to a particular section of the book and, hopefully, find something to inspire, motivate, or otherwise help. **Please browse** if you simply don't feel like you can stand reading back to front. **Strategies and tools are set in bold text,** so hopefully, you'll be able to spot something you can use.

Section I has six broad principles that can be applied to all your issues, and Section II brings you into a number of classic ADHD challenge areas. Woven into both sections are tools and strategies that address each challenge.

SIMPLE PRINCIPLES TO GO BY

ADHDers Have Amazing Abilities, So Getting a Grip on Your Challenges is Worth It

Beyond the very real challenges of ADHD is a person who's authentic, creative, innovative, intuitive, and very bright.

In my world, **ADHD women are the ones with the juice**! I'm always attracted to them as friends. I love the fluidity of their minds, their intuition, their out-of-the box creativity, the fact that they can fly all over the place and not lose a strand of the communication. I love that they're full of ideas and grasp connections and patterns others don't see – instantly synthesizing related issues. I love their ability to brainstorm the heck out of anything. Our world is full of ADHDers, and it's richer because of them. They're great talkers, artists, inventors, innovators, comedians, and deep thinkers.

I once had a remarkable therapist who had ADHD. I have to say, she was almost always late (although she would call my cell to alert me and apologize). But I never minded waiting for her because she was so good. At the end of our first session, she sort of summed up what she'd heard me say – the ground I'd covered. And what she'd understood from what I'd said was much more complex, contextual, and complete than I'd thought I'd communicated. I saw then, in a flash, how highly intuitive she was and what a valuable gift that is. She was that way in all our sessions and she helped me a lot. And, I've seen this same skill in many other women with ADHD.

Which isn't to say that having ADHD is not a tough row to hoe. Having to work hard at tasks others do with little effort can feel like swimming upstream. **It's also difficult in that most people who don't have ADHD can't really understand it, or you:** Trying to explain why you haven't done your taxes for another week, when you promised you would, doesn't engender sympathy or even comprehension from others. **ADHD is a real, brain-based problem that makes it hard to get your focus center engaged or moving fluidly.** Sadly, people who are uneducated about ADHD simply can't understand, when you neglect doing something, the way they would understand if you had the flu, or God forbid, a more serious physical illness. Still, as we educate ourselves about attention deficit we can teach our friends and families about it, too. And, best of all, we can harness our energies so our lives are easier by using tools like the ones in this book.

The challenges ADHDers face, they share with world-class talents, like musicians Justin Timberlake and Solange Knowles, acclaimed journalists Lisa Ling and Katherine Ellison, Olympians Michael Phelps and Cammi Granato, entrepreneurs Paul Orfalea (founder of Kinko's) and Richard Branson (Virgin Atlantic.) Evidence suggests that greats like Galileo, Thomas Edison, Agatha Christie, and Virginia Woolf probably had ADHD, too.

There's so much that's exceptional, rich, and valuable in people with ADHD, that the rewards of working on managing the hard parts of it are big.

Keep Things Simple

I do best by keeping things as simple as I can, which, in this world, almost sounds like a joke! Still, there are ways to keep our lives simpler and ways to **impose boundaries around various tasks, efforts, things, spaces, and time** that help us better direct, use, and focus our fantastically curious abilities to pay attention.

Having fewer options helps me simplify. Fewer clothes, for instance, makes deciding what to wear easier. I cook quite a bit and I've learned to **pare down the number of gadgets and even the skillets, pots, and pans** that I have. **Getting rid of old photos and organizing the ones I want** is turning out to be a formidable task, but I'm working up to it! (I want digital photos I can find with ease, not boxes full of pictures I never look at.) I have **fewer sheets**: two sets for each bed and a couple extras for guests. I used to have a jumble of them, which would be no problem for someone who wasn't bothered by jumbles, but I am.

You can also simplify your life by **scheduling various repetitive tasks for the same time and day each week**. This way, you won't have to struggle deciding whether or when to go grocery shopping, you'll have the day set in stone. It'll probably be hard to stay with your commitment in the beginning (you could change your mind about it being a good idea!). But, if you can imagine that committing to a set time for a particular weekly task could help you – and you choose to work with it – make it your everything for a couple months. By that I mean, nurture the effort by giving it an enhanced sense of importance in your mind and use just this one tool until it becomes a habit. **This is how I've had to work with each strategy I've implemented: one at a time, one day at a time, until the thing becomes automatic**.

Managing ADHD on a daily basis means that we have to work at life skills that most folks take for granted. **Culling extraneous things from your living space and assigning homes to everything** requires a big effort. But if you can do it, you won't have to decide where to shove things every time you're straightening up: they will have a home so you can just put them back there. Easy.

Each of the tools in the next section of this book should help you simplify some area of your life so you can manage things more easily. Don't forget to **keep it simple even when choosing a tool**: Don't let the tool become more complicated than the problem! You might want to start with the tool that appeals to you most and work at using it until it's working for you.

Let Perfection Go

I have a friend who is very good at recognizing when she needs help. Unfortunately, she usually decides that the "right" person – the one who could really help – is a high-profile national expert who's not local, not taking clients, or too expensive. The result? She ends up not getting help, even though there are plenty of suitable practitioners right in her hometown who could work with her tomorrow.

Perfectionism like this is a mind trick that keeps you stuck. It's very useful to **remember to start where you are, with what you have.**

Don't look for the perfect technique, diet, outfit, job, schedule, or system. It's an impossible standard. Look for the one that you can use, get, buy, afford, call, or understand now.

Ask for Help: Find an ADHD Buddy, Professional Coach, or Other Social Support

A fascinating article by the journalist David Dobbs in the December 2009 issue of The Atlantic confirmed and validated something I've experienced and observed in others and myself for years.

The article presents a new hypothesis that researchers are exploring concerning people who have genes that make them prone to ADHD, depression, anxiety, and/or other difficult issues. Part of the researchers' previous thinking about the "bad" genes is that they only manifest in negative experience and behavior *if they get activated by stressful experiences*. It's a very interesting validation that nature and nurture both affect us.

The new theory, however, takes the understanding of these genes' sensitivity to nurture in a very constructive and hopeful direction.

It posits that these particular genetic vulnerabilities are not only susceptible to the effects of negative life experiences but also have a heightened sensitivity and response to positive experiences.

What the researchers found is that those of us with these genetic sensitivities respond exceedingly well to positive influences. In fact, positive interventions (in other words, help) allow people with genetic vulnerabilities like ADHD to excel *beyond* people who don't have the same genetic markers!

They call it the Orchid Effect because orchids, unlike heartier plants, are highly sensitive and don't thrive without good nurturing. Orchids will, however, bloom fantastically if given good care, creating a vast range of extraordinary blossoms that retain their beauty for months.

What this means to me – and what I've experienced – is that **women with ADHD can excel beyond an average person without ADHD – *when they have help*.**

Don't isolate. Don't let shame get you. Have the brave vulnerability of the truly courageous and **ask for help**.

I've sought out help and support in several ways. I've had talking therapists. I've had a therapist who worked with me as an **ADHD coach,** helping me sort things out, set strategies in motion, and stick with them. I've had an **ADHD buddy** – who is, incidentally, a college professor. We'd meet weekly or bi-weekly and talk about our issues and progress. And I ask friends and family members for help often. Lots of times, when I'm stuck, even a little connection – talking or texting – is enough to encourage or motivate me again. And people are happy to help.

Take Care of Your Whole Self

No matter what your most challenging issues are, taking good care of yourself helps.

The brain is part of the body, so **whatever you do to nourish and exercise your body will help alleviate your symptoms.**

I'm not a doctor, but any mom or teacher can tell you: eating a sugary breakfast (or skipping breakfast entirely) will kill your concentration. Research reveals carbohydrates, especially gluten, to be highly suspect as responsible for brain fog and worse. Learn what's best for you to eat and start to make those changes. A nourished brain works better.

Regular exercise, preferably outside, really helps. Study after study finds that exercise is a first-line treatment for ADHD and related issues.

Why outside? It's called the "Green-Time Effect." **Spending time in nature** significantly reduces kids' ADHD symptoms. It will work for you, too. Even if you can't exercise outdoors, step out whenever you can. Jane McGonigall cites evidence in her book *Superbetter*, that even looking out a window for 30 seconds increases your inner resilience. It's powerful stuff.

Above all, **you must sleep**. Sleep deprivation causes ADHD symptoms all by itself. It slows your reaction time as much as being legally drunk. Some experts say that losing just an hour of sleep a day for one week will lower your IQ! Can you afford that? I can't.

When you're rested, you concentrate and remember better. You'll have more energy and impulse control, so you'll eat better, exercise more, feel less stressed, and have an easier time managing your weight.

Depending on how severe your symptoms are, **seek support from an experienced psychiatrist or psychopharmacologist to explore whether you might do well on medication**. It doesn't work for everybody, but it can help some people a lot. Interestingly, I can't tolerate even the lowest dose of Adderall, one of the main ADHD meds: I get way too speedy and then crash heavily. But I am lucky enough to have a psychopharmacologist who recognizes that **off-the-label dosing can be effective**. Many days, I open an Adderall cap, and carefully pour out 15 grains. You practically need a magnifying glass to count them. But that miniscule dose helps me. I'm guessing an Adderall cap has 200-300 grains ... so it doesn't seem believable that one capsule can last me weeks and weeks, but it's true.

Build a Custom Toolbox: Take What You Can Use from This Book and Don't Worry About the Rest

Tools – tactics, structure, and support – are key to getting a grip on yourself and creating a balanced life.

Everybody is wired a little differently: ADHDers don't all have the same set of challenges.

For example, I've got ADHD symptoms up the wazoo, yet I'm not chronically late, I don't lose my keys and phone, and I never simply forget a meeting. One of my best friends, however, cannot, just cannot, use a to do list in a little notebook because she can't hold on to the notebook. Another fun, loving, highly successful businesswoman friend is always late. I know she works hard at this and feels badly about it, but it still plagues her.

So, although we both have ADHD, and share several issues, we don't share several others. She doesn't struggle with indecisiveness like I do, getting zoned completely out in large stores, or having difficulty staying in touch with friends and family.

Your challenges will be just as individual, so **when you look through the tools in this book, just pick one that jumps out at you. Try it, and if it helps, stick with it.** Soon you'll see it improving other areas of your life, too. Ultimately, you'll develop your own personal group of tools that work together in a strong, resilient system.

Accept It

Look, just about everybody's got something. This is earth. At least we can work on ADHD. Besides, **acceptance removes the extra layer of negative**

energy that makes everything harder. Acceptance makes focusing on solutions easier because you don't have to fight your self-pity, resentment, or any other form of negativity surrounding your difficulties. Therapists, coaches, ADHD buddies, or friends can help you work on accepting your hard parts.

CHALLENGING AREAS AND HELPFUL WAYS AROUND THEM:

Tools, Strategies, Structures, and Other Supports

Difficulty Prioritizing

I was first diagnosed with ADHD by a therapist who suddenly said to me, after a year, Oh, My God, Joni: You have ADHD: You can't tell the difference between what's really important to you and what's not!

And, he was right. If I'm off the beam, it's easy for me to devote as much energy to unimportant things as I do on things that are very important to me. Which is not how I want to spend my life.

What's important in life? That's very individual, but the late, great time management guru Stephen Covey has outlined some principles that help clarify the issue by **identifying the differences between things that are important and things that are urgent**. Too often, I'll confuse the two.

Important things are the things that, if accomplished, will lead to you achieving what you truly value and want to build with your life: Things that, on your death bed, you'll be proud of or grateful for having been able to do.

Urgent things can and most often are unimportant – in the sense that they won't amount to anything meaningful: taking all afternoon waiting in line at the DMV to renew your license because you didn't mail it in, for instance.

The only way to spend your energy on important things is to begin by identifying your priorities.

Priorities work on a lifetime level, and a daily level.

Lifetime priorities are the things that are most important to you for the current season or year or even longer: being loving to your family and friends, perhaps; taking care of your health; working on your ADHD; financial planning; applying to grad school; etc.

Yet, even if a person has identified their lifetime priorities, many fail to achieve them because they can't establish their daily priorities. To do this, you have to **deconstruct your lifetime priorities into the small, action steps that you can take on a daily basis to accomplish them.**

Breaking things down into small steps is a fundamental human tool that ADHDers often have a hard time doing naturally.

Without being able to identify daily priorities, people end up bouncing around like ping pong balls responding to whatever appears in front of them. If a friend calls, they can't not answer the phone. If they suddenly think they must have new throw pillows, they can't resist dropping everything to go shopping. Because they've avoided taking care of paperwork and bills, or paying attention to loved ones' birthdays or other needs, they end up in crazy, urgent rushes doing whatever it is they've neglected. It's called putting out fires. Interestingly, many of us are very effective at putting out fires – largely because the task at hand is so clear-cut it sharpens the focus and we can feel the peace of one-pointed concentration.

Not only that, but many people with ADHD like the stimulation of a speedy chase.

No one seems to know where the following story originated. I've read it in several places, including Stephen Covey's book, *First Things First*. In any case, it graphically illustrates how important priorities are and how daily priorities depend on having identified your big, lifetime priorities: those values, goals, and things that are most important to you.

So, the story goes that a teacher stands in front of his students with a big gallon sized glass jar into which he places several large rocks until the jar can't take anymore. At that point, he asks the class if the jar is full.

'Yes, yes, of course,' answer the students, at which point the smiling teacher pours in a few cups of smaller rocks, jiggling the jar until they have filled in the spaces around the large rocks. At that point, he again asks the class if the jar is full.

Suddenly hip to the teacher, they all say no. At which point, he pours some sand into the jar, which filters down and fills in the empty spaces among the big and small rocks. At that point he, again, asks the class if the jar is full. Knowing what they will answer, he begins filling the jar with water and asks again, if the jar is full. To which everybody yells, 'Yes, it's full now!'

The moral: You've got to get your big rocks (most important things) in place first or you won't be able to fit them into your life.

Still, **prioritizing can be really hard for people with ADHD, so don't hesitate to seek help.** You can find it in many ways, depending on how you operate. As always, ADHD coaches can really help. So can ADHD buddies, friends, and family members who are naturally good at prioritizing or have learned how. **Books on goal setting can help.** If books aren't easy for you, **search for audiobooks, podcasts, or Ted talks on prioritizing,** or goal setting. **If the Internet is daunting for you, get someone to help you do this.**

Getting Distracted and Sidetracked

Ever have one of those songs that just won't stop going around and around your head?

Your brain is wired to obsess over unresolved issues. When you have something you need to remember, or an idea you want to pursue but you haven't acted on it, it creates an open loop that nags at you and congests your thinking.

If, however, you **capture the thought in a safe place you can access later,** it frees your mind and your attention for whatever you want to pay attention to at the time.

Your Capture System needs to be something you will always keep with you, and that you can add and retrieve info to and from effortlessly. For me that's words, so I like to use what I call a **desk notebook**. I date each desk notebook on the cover (with masking tape or a fancy label from a labeler). I keep it either on my desk, or in my bag, and I write everything, everything, in it as messily as I want: what the Comcast guy said on the phone; people's phone numbers; appointments; names of movies and books; a website I've heard about, anything. And,

here's another important part of using the desk notebook: You have to open it and look at what you've written in there several times a day. If you don't, you'll start to want to jot things down other places and get turned off to the notebook. I also go through the notebook, periodically, and transfer important information to other more localized places, like my computer, phone, or paper address book and calendar. But, even if I don't transfer the information, it's always there in the desk notebook so I can always refer back to it. When I fill one notebook up, I start a new one, but keep the old one. The thing that makes it work is always, always, using it. Anything you'd put on a scrap of paper, put in your notebook instead.

If a notebook doesn't work for you, maybe you can **use a notes app on your smart phone that backs up to your computer**. Mac Notes allows you to add things to it either from your smart phone or your Mac – and the cloud syncs them up. I'm sure PCs have similar apps, or use Google docs.

If you're visual, you can capture ideas with the camera on your smart phone. Your **phone's camera is such a cool little tool for capturing info**: in a hurry you can take a picture of a written notice, or a business card, or a poem you like in a book somewhere. Or, try Pinterest: You can upload snapshots of things you want to remember, group them by topic, search by name, and make them private so no one sees them but you.

If you think out loud, use **voice notes**. Google Voice will even transcribe what you say and save it directly to your online drive. If you like all of the above, a program like **Evernote** can collect many different formats. The important thing is that you use your system, and you trust it. When you trust your system, you'll get great peace of mind from using it.

Difficulty Following Through and Staying Motivated

Many of us fail to follow through on a project we were so excited about yesterday. Whatever the reason, neglecting to follow through repeatedly makes it really hard to believe that you can do anything – and that erodes self-esteem. It's critical to follow through on projects.

A common reason we abandon a project is lagging excitement over it, so **we need to find ways to get and stay motivated, focused, engaged, and stimulated**.

Music can help. Compile a bunch of tunes that get you up and jumping, then tackle the project.

Often, **setting a timer for a short period** – like eight minutes – helps me get started on something I don't want to do. I'll say to myself that I'm only going to work on the thing for eight minutes. Creating a (short) time limit lessens my resistance to starting. And, more often than not, once the time is up, I'm engaged and want to continue working. But, if I don't want to continue, I keep my word to myself and stop (so I'll trust myself the next time I want to use a timer).

For getting certain things done, like housework (ugh!), I let myself take advantage of my natural inclination to bounce from one thing to another. I had several jobs as a waitress way back, and I was good at it! Fast, fast, fast! The job is full of urgency: get this person this, get that person that! You're so busy, you fly through the restaurant, making every step count: If you've gotten a request for a side of mayo and are headed to the kitchen, you pick up any dirty dishes on the way. In the kitchen, while getting the mayo, you grab a side plate you know Table 5 is going to need when their next course is up. On route to deliver the mayo and plate, you stop to see if Table 4 likes their appetizers.

So, this is how I straighten up the house: Music blaring, I bounce from room to room. Say I start by taking laundry to the washing machine. While I'm there, I'll pick up some towels that belong in the upstairs bathroom. Upstairs, I'll see that the towel cabinet is messy and empty it out and straighten it up. Liking the way it feels to see the cabinet orderly motivates me to clean the top bathroom drawer, so I do. Having the sponge out for the drawer, I scrub the tub and the sink. Taking the waste paper basket downstairs to empty, I grab some scissors that belong in the kitchen and put them away. In the kitchen, I set the timer for eight minutes, and start cleaning. I've actually developed an order to cleaning the kitchen that works for me (and may be painfully obvious to people without ADHD!). No matter how long I'm going to devote to cleaning the kitchen, I always start by putting away the dishes in the drying rack or dishwasher, so I'll have places to put the dirty things later. I may just do those two tasks, and leave the kitchen. But, if I beat the clock, I start washing dishes. When my watch goes off, and I'm not finished, I may set the clock for another eight minutes, and keep going – or not. When the kitchen's done – or I want to move on – I grab a few magazines from the kitchen table and take them upstairs where I keep a pile of them. I end up getting a lot done this way; I just have to be careful not to throw out anything important in my quasi-mania!

Connecting with someone before starting your project can also remove resistance to resuming work on a project you want to abandon. **Make a quick phone call to an ADHD-friendly friend,** or your ADHD buddy, and say you're starting the project and that you're going to call them when you finish. Then call them when you finish. This **"bookending"** technique is so useful. For some of us with ADHD, **connecting with others, even briefly, buoys the spirit and gets us going**. Telling someone what you're intending to do keeps you accountable and gives you a psychological sense that someone is in it with you. ADHDers respond wildly well to palpable support like this.

It's also useful to **post images, meaningful quotes, and positive messages to inspire you**. You can do this with paper, on your phone or computer, or both.

Understanding and accepting that follow through is important and will lead to the next right step, marshal all your resources to finish what you start. At least most of the time. (If something was really a poor idea, let it go.)

Sometimes we allow urgent tasks to put us off continuing work on our project. Sometimes those tasks are urgent, but sometimes they just feel urgent. Urgency is stimulating and easy because what you've got to do is clear cut: pick up your kid five towns away or get the oil light on your dash to go off. Don't fall for it if you can put it off for an hour: Remember that your project is important to your health.

If neglecting to follow through is simply a matter of losing track of all your many projects, then **automated reminders** might work well for you. You can set up notifications on your phone calendar, pre-scheduled emails, or task-list programs. **Some online Capture Systems, like Evernote, have a reminder function built in**. Use your reminders to prompt motivation, not just memory – linking to images, meaningful quotes, or positive messages that will keep you from just swiping those notifications away.

If you prefer paper over digital, try an old-school "tickler" file. Set up an index-card box or Pendaflex sorter labeled 1-31 and January-December, and you can pop in messages to your future self. (Of course, you have to remember to check the folders!) Here again, make the reminder engaging and inspiring so you don't just skip over it. Photo postcards, quote-a-day or cartoon-a-day calendars work great for this, too.

The things that create quality of life and help us achieve our goals don't bonk us on the head: personal growth, self-care, self-awareness, cultivating helpful habits, lifelong learning, creative expression, deep relationships. Learning how to motivate yourself will help in all areas of your life.

Losing Things

When I worked in the theater, I loved seeing the stage manager set up the props for a show. They'd lay everything out on a long table and outline each thing in colored tape. Every nifty shape had its own label: Act I Letter; Act II Rose; Act III Revolver. They each had a dedicated space and were very specific, because a missing prop could send the whole play off the rails.

You may not want to cover your table with tape, but you can **dedicate and assign a space for your wandering possessions**. And, then, you can simply return them to where they belong when they "escape." Over time they will come to like their home and stay there more often. After losing my phone a bunch of times, I decided to have it live in a slot pocket in a cross-body bag. At first, it took some doing to remember to keep putting it there, but now it's habitual. Sometimes I'll still think I've lost track of it, and almost all the time I'll find it in its pocket. Now, if I want a new bag, I have to get one with a similar slot. It's that important to me.

When you have to make a decision about every stray sock or scrap of paper you pick up, it's exhausting. That's when we become overwhelmed, our homes get cluttered, and we can't find anything. Make those decisions ahead of time, so when you pick something up you don't have to think about where it goes.

Some items have a single function or you use them in a single place, like a 3-hole punch or a shower scrubbie. You only need one of these that "lives" in a dedicated spot.

For things you use in multiple places and for multiple purposes, buy duplicates and keep them everywhere you use them – like cleaning supplies, business cards, or pens. Plenty of people buy multiple pairs of cheap reading glasses and keep one in every room of the house.

A launch pad by the door, for gathering things you want to remember to take with you, works great for some people. I have a friend, though, who will walk right past it! Instead, **she tapes lists right to the glass on the door, or hangs a bag from the knob.** You can write yourself notes in dry-erase marker on glass or mirrors, too. Be creative about designing your space!

You can design your schedule, too, by doing things at the same time each week. This creates a rhythm: a balanced, habitual series of actions that flow together naturally. Rhythm keeps routine maintenance from piling up behind your back. A simple rhythm would be cleaning the house, the bathroom, or doing the laundry on the same day every week.

Here's another example: I have obligations every Sunday, Tuesday, and Wednesday. I know I'll be out of the house, and in a certain part of town, so I stack nearby errands around those appointments: the bank, the fish market, the grocery store. My Capture System (my notebook) keeps track of what I need to buy or do while I'm there, so I'm all set.

This structure feels good and makes it easier to decide how to plan other activities around the schedule I've set in place.

A weekly rhythm cuts down worry and distractions, too. When I notice something needs doing, I can pretty easily figure out when I will have time to take care of it.

It's simple to start. Just jot down your existing commitments with other people (those are probably the ones you keep most regularly) – classes, deadlines, social events. Think about where you'll be, and how you'll feel – and what you can add on to do while you are wherever it is that you'll be.

Before you know it, you'll feel your daily and weekly rhythms supporting you in all kinds of ways.

Chronic Lateness

One friend, a highly successful businesswoman, is always late. I've seen her in action and it's fascinating. We might be racing to make it to an event we both really want to go to when she suddenly decides she wants an iced tea. It's as though she steps into an alternate reality where time doesn't exist as she casually looks for her good citrus juicer to squeeze a lemon, searches for her favorite travel cup, etc., having apparently forgotten our time squeeze.

Some people avoid timers because they feel stressed and rushed. But losing track of time results in undone work and missed deadlines (like collecting your kids from school). It's beyond stressful and it can have painful consequences for the people you care about.

Forget the timer on your phone and absolutely **invest in a watch that will accommodate multiple alarms and timers and learn how to use it with ease**. Soon, if you're like me, you'll love it.

When you start an absorbing task – whether it's creative work or clearing closets – decide when to take a break. Even with several hours of work ahead, regular breaks keep your body limber and your mind refreshed. Ten or 15 minutes every hour is a good rule of thumb, so set your timer in 45-minute increments. When it goes off, stretch, drink some water, and check your to-do list. Your productivity will skyrocket – just be sure to time your break, too!

For deadlines like leaving for a meeting, **set your alarm with time to spare**. Don't set it for the time you need to leave, but for the time you need to get ready to leave. Then you have permission to do anything until it goes off – not watching the clock. That permission is so freeing, you might start to really love using timers.

For dreaded, mundane busywork like housework, filing, paperwork, or possibly exercise, use your timer for motivation. Play "Let's Make a Deal" (you only have to gut it out for a short time), or "Beat the Clock" (how much can you get done before the ding?) Be sure to celebrate your win.

Many workout apps will coach you in interval training or simple routines – just follow the friendly voice. If you're like me, exercise is way more fun when you don't have to think about it.

Ready to get advanced? "Supersets" will supercharge your day! Check your to-do list. Some jobs need extended focus. Others can be done in short chunks. Use your short tasks as breaks from your longer ones. Think about the value of creating rhythm and alternate high and low energy activities for maximum benefit.

Difficulty Making Decisions and Choices

Everything you do requires decision-making. Tea or coffee? Do you want to get a masters degree? Study languages or guitar? Become a parent or remain childless? When you're stuck, small decisions are as hard as big ones.

Difficulty deciding is the root of many ADHD challenges. Often, the thing that diverts us from following through – even if we're not aware of it at the time – is a decision, or a string of them. Even when you do know what you want, you have to figure out how to make it happen – and then you have a whole decision-tree of options and contingencies!

Say you want to put up shelves. You gather the tools, including your husband's stud finder (which you don't actually know how to use, which throws a little starting wrench in your mental works). Then, you begin wondering if the shelves are worth having to patch the nail holes when you move. And, by the way, are you going to renew your lease? And, is this the best wall for shelves? And on and on it goes. These issues may never emerge into consciousness, but they leave you with a congested feeling that builds and builds. And the shelves don't go up.

The age-old simple technique of **listing the Pros and Cons of any decision is very helpful.** On the left side of a piece of paper write Pros and on the right side write Cons. Then, starting with the Pros, write down all the positives you believe will result from doing the thing in question. Take time with this, and think it through. Then, under Cons, list all the negatives you think will result from doing the thing in question. Often, this clarifies what you really want to do.

Meanwhile, it's always helpful to **springboard your feelings off someone you trust**. Others can see things we can't, help organize the steps involved, and raise factors we may not have considered. Supportive people can help us find clarity. Don't substitute other people's judgment for your own, but your response for or against a piece of advice can make your real desires crystal clear.

Lucky for me, I have a close friend who is particularly clear-minded about making decisions, and finding solutions. When I texted her for help deciding between the iPhone 6 or the Plus, she answered, "Make a list of pros and cons, but remember you're going to be somewhat dissatisfied with either one, because nothing is perfect." It was simple advice, but I needed it and it helped me.

Crowd-sourcing minor decisions is a fun and productive way to use your social media networks. Asking your friends to weigh in on issues you're having to decide can be helpful.

Connecting honestly about our challenges with people we trust deepens authentic friendships. And, it's so true that helping someone helps the giver as much as the receiver.

Feeling Overwhelmed

I'd venture a guess that most people, when they walk into a café, let's say, focus largely on finding a free table. Of course, depending on the person, they'll also take in the pastry case, the barista, where the line forms for coffee.

But many people with ADHD will walk into that same café and, in the first two minutes, see all those things but also have become aware of a young couple on a first date; an older single woman reading Shakespeare; the fact that the barista has just been rude to the customer in front of him; that the owner just gave the barista a disapproving look; that the floors have been refinished recently; that a girl with a baby is depressed; that the heat doesn't work well in the place; and much, much more.

This is the way some ADHDers' perception works. They see a lot. They don't choose to, it's just the way their focus is. It's quick and wide. And, not only that, but many feel pressure to respond in some way to all they see. This sensory overload results in feeling overwhelmed and makes it a chore to stay focused on the activity at hand.

And that's just ordering coffee. You want to clean out your garage or do your taxes? Eeek! It's all just too much, so we shut down. Then all those overwhelming, undone jobs pile up and create chaos, clutter, and all sorts of penalties – physical, financial, and emotional.

One way to offload some level of overwhelm, is to do what we'll call a brain dump. Take your desk notebook (or whatever you use to write in), and just let it rip with all the things that you think you should do, want to do, or have to do. It doesn't matter if they're as different as picking up the dry cleaning and finding a long-lost relative. Keep writing. Keep writing. Write down every little thing that weighs on you – everything. Don't stop until you simply cannot think of one more thing. I find this a big relief in and of itself. But you can make further use of it, by reviewing it later and seeing what it is on the list that you need to do first, what the longer term goals are, what you need extra help with, etc. You can do a brain dump every day if you want, once a week, or whenever you feel the need.

In terms of your workload, be creative with your resources and **outsource some of the chores** you like the least so you can spend your energy focusing on your strengths. The freed-up time and energy, and improved results, will make a net positive to your peace of mind and your bottom line.

If meal planning is a pain for you, try a subscription that emails you menus and grocery lists.

If housecleaning and yard work are a constant hassle, see if you can budget for a cleaning service and lawn care help.

Asking for help like this doesn't mean just paid help. Are your kids doing age-appropriate chores? Even little ones can match socks. Kids (even if they're not your own) love to earn pocket money for extra jobs around the house.

If you're someone who does too much for others, **learning to say no** can be healthy and helpful. If this is a big issue for you, seek help with it.

Some people, no matter how much help they have, still feel overwhelmed. It's a common side effect of the digital age. **Learning to stay present is an age-old practice**. Staying present means to consciously check in and observe what you're focusing on and then gently retrain your focus to observe what you're actually doing at that moment. If it's ordering coffee from a girl, focus on the girl: look her in the eye, smile, take a breath, and realize you're there at a café counter! If it's washing dishes, look at your hands, the water, feel the warmth, breathe: I am here. This type of practice can be called mindfulness. As they say in 12 Step programs, **keep your head where your feet are.**

This is a worthwhile, lifelong challenge for almost anyone – meditation teachers, monks, and regular people alike. And it can be doubling difficult for some people with ADHD – and doubly rewarding.

Any type of **meditation, too, helps** calm us down and alleviates the stress of feeling overwhelmed, **but if meditation sounds daunting, just forget it, and sit quietly by yourself** for one, five, or 10 minutes instead. This quiet communion with yourself will help establish an inner awareness of your own awareness – and what it's focused on. If you keep at it, it will help you develop the concentration to remember to keep your head where your feet are, if even only for minutes at a time. Minutes at a time is great and will help you immeasurably.

There are many helpful books, podcasts, and You Tube videos on mindfulness and various forms of meditation. Writing in a journal can be a great help, too. **Once you start on a path, all kinds of resources will pop up.**

Impulsivity

ADHDers don't just see and feel a lot, they feel drawn to respond and do something about all they see. Tremendous curiosity over new ideas and possibilities can feel so exciting, so sure a thing! This momentary excitement can feel so strong, you can do something before you've thought it through: Invited someone over for dinner; sent an email saying things you wish you hadn't; bought a puppy! Morning coffee is an especially impulsive time for me, and I've learned not to let myself make any decisions until later in the day. But that alone doesn't ensure that I won't do something impulsive.

Every situation has so many possibilities, but not all of those possibilities are productive or helpful. Oh, but they are so attractive! Every idea, sense, person, and opportunity can set off passionate curiosity or strong reactions. The result? Wasted time, extra pounds, financial strain, and words you can't take back.

Willpower is a limited commodity. Consciously saying "no" to unhelpful impulses creates decision fatigue. Over time, that mental tiredness undermines your goal, whether it's time management, finishing a difficult bit of work, or putting down the Haagen Dazs. When you're not in the throes of an impulse, **set up reasonable limits and engineer yourself into good choices,** so you don't have to constantly face and reject temptation.

If social media and the Internet are calling your name, **install blocking software**. Many free apps will turn off certain sites – or the whole Internet – on a programmed schedule.

For a noisy, busy work environment, **try noise-cancelling headphones, or a white-noise soundtrack**. I like to use **"binaural beat" music**, which is supposed to sync your brainwaves to a focused state. I've got no scientific proof, but it helps me.

Visual clutter and works-in-progress drag you off track. Clear your workspace when it's time to focus, even if that means sweeping everything into a bin to be dealt with later.

If the sudden hungries blow your healthy eating plan, pre-portion your snacks for the day, and put physical distance between yourself and the junk. When I started working from home, I had a standing desk installed in the kitchen. I quickly put on 10 pounds. Now my workspace is in a back bedroom, and I can't mindlessly snack.

Remember, make desired behavior easy. Make undesired behavior as hard as possible.

Procrastination: Not Wanting to Do Whatever It Is

Everybody procrastinates to some extent, but some of us have a seriously difficult and apparently inexplicable time getting down to doing certain tasks. This is sadly misunderstood as a matter of poor will power by those who haven't taken the time to learn about ADHD. But, will power doesn't come into it. It's a problem in the brain's management system.

I can go weeks not getting to something I've identified as a priority: something that's really important to me. I'll have written it in my desk notebook, thought about it quite a bit and, still, each day will go by and I don't do it. I see the task I want to do – as time passes – as a distant image. **My abilities to focus on it and my abilities to take action just won't connect**.

On the other hand, I can easily fly through tasks and activities I like.

This is probably the least understood aspect of ADHD: "Sure," people think who are ignorant about ADHD, "She just doesn't want to do the hard stuff! I don't want to do it either, but I just do it!"

Being unable to turn on our focus centers and "just do it" is rough and causes a lot of painful, anxiety-provoking procrastination that weighs us down.

There are many factors involved in procrastination – which is good news. It means that **there are various techniques to disrupt the web of behaviors that keep you stuck**. Almost any tool in this book will help procrastination, either directly or indirectly. It's like that old song, "The hip bone's connected to the thigh bone, the thigh bone's connected to the knee bone ..." By that I mean, that as you implement strategies and get a better handle on a particular challenge, it becomes easier to get a handle on any other ADHD challenge, including procrastination.

Conventional wisdom advises rewarding yourself when you reach a goal. That's great, but for most ADHDers, the "pain" of a boring or overwhelming task is right there in your face, while the future "gain" of the reward seems abstract and far away. **Use your creativity to make the task itself rewarding!** As Mary Poppins says, "a spoonful of sugar helps the medicine go down." However dreary or emotionally fraught the job, there is some way to sweeten the deal, engage your focus center, and push you through the inertia.

Keep yourself stimulated during rote work with music, an audiobook, or podcast. Or **call a friend** to talk you through it. If social support is really helpful for you, you could **ask a friend to come sit with you**, or set up **regular dates with your "study buddy."**

You have five senses, and infinite ways to combine them with most tasks. Don't be afraid to be eccentric! Rewards while you work can be anything from your favorite tea or a rocking playlist, to soaking your feet or wearing a silly hat. Whatever puts a smile on your face will make a task that much easier to start.

FINAL WORDS

I made this small book as simple as possible so it'd be easy-ish – for someone who felt overwhelmed by the idea of reading a book on ADHD – to open to any page and get something useful out of it. I always feel a little lift of encouragement whenever I have even a little win, so I've learned how something small can build into something big. If you find a single tool here that works for you, remember that there are experts, clinicians, books, websites, podcasts, and articles that can deepen your working knowledge of it.

I've never published on Amazon before. As a journalist, it's been difficult to believe that self-publishing was legit (I've always believed that only a publishing house or newspaper or magazine can produce valuable content). But the changes in the newspaper and magazine industries I've seen in the last decade prompted me to explore Kindle publishing. I've learned a lot about it and been wanting to try it for a while now. As simple as this booklet is, it's been hard for me to believe in it and stick with it – for all sorts of reasons (many of which are covered in this book!). But putting down on "paper" all the issues that I've struggled with, with ADHD, helped me to see how important it is to finish projects I start. And, I'm so happy I have because the process of overcoming various doubts about doing it has helped me push through on other fronts when I feel rebuffed by my own conflicting and fickle enthusiasms. Not only that, but by learning what I've had to learn to get this piece up on Amazon and market it, a door has opened to other ideas I very much want to write about. And that flow feels hopeful and good.

Thanks so much for buying the book. If you feel like leaving a review on Amazon, I'd really appreciate it. The more reviews and sales a Kindle book has, the higher up Amazon ranks it. And, the higher a book is ranked, the more people there are who will see it. And, the more people who see it, the more people there are who just might click that magical little BUY NOW button!

Please feel free to email me at joan.wilder@gmail.com – I'd be thrilled to hear from any readers.

Also, please visit my new blog Help for Women with ADHD at HelpForWomenWithADHD.com and let me know what's going on with you.

OTHER RESOURCES

For more help, you might find one or more of the following books, sites, or social media accounts useful:

Books

Delivered from Distraction, Edward M. Hallowell and John J. Ratey, Ballantine Books, 2006. A strengths-based approach to overcoming ADHD challenges by a pioneer in the field. Hallowell has ADHD and a very compassionate positive take on it.

Fast Minds, Craig Surman and Tim Bilkey with Karen Weintraub, Berkley Books, 2013. Understand your collection of intense traits and how to harness them positively.

Healing ADHD Revised Edition: The Breakthrough Program that Allows You to See

and Heal the 7 Types of ADHD, Daniel G. Amen, Berkley Books, 2013. Recognize and address different manifestations of ADHD, including very specific nutritional recommendations.

Queen of Distraction, Terry Matlen and Sari Solden, New Harbinger Publications, 2014. This is a great book with lots of personal experience and strategies for women with ADHD from an ADHD coach.

True Refuge: Finding Peace and Freedom in Your Own Awakened Heart, Random House, Tara Brach, LLC, 2013. A beautiful book on the gifts of being present to both pain and joy from a mindfulness meditation teacher and therapist.

Radical Acceptance: Embracing Your Life With The Heart of A Buddha, Tara Brach, Random House LLC, 2004. Another beautiful book from Tara about awakening into the present from the trance of unworthiness many of us experience.

Websites, apps, blogs

Attention Deficit Disorder, The official Open Group on Facebook. This is a great place to share feelings and tools about living with ADHD.

Kaleidoscopesociety.com. This is a website with stories about and by women with ADHD. You can also find them on Instagram.

Instagram.com/ADHD.problems, an Instagram page. A lot of fun, useful, and funny stuff.

Instagram.com/ADHD_life, another Instagram page with interesting and inspirational ideas.

Instagram.com/thetruthaboutadhd, another Instagram page to check out.

AddConsults.com. This is Terry Matlen's web site. Terry is a psychotherapist, ADHD coach, and the author of Queen of Distraction.

Flylady.net. The queen of email reminders for organizing your life.

ADDitudeMag.com. ADD-itude Magazine delivers new articles every month on scientific and real-life topics pertaining to ADHD challenges.

Evernote.com. Billed as "the workspace for your life's work." Collect notes, reminders, and files in many different media and sync between your phone and desktop.

Tarabrach.com. Dozens of lovely, guided, mindfulness meditation talks. Tara is the founder of Insight Meditation outside Washington, D.C. and is also a therapist. (You can also put this site on your smart phone.)

ABOUT THE AUTHOR

As a freelance journalist, Joan Wilder has written hundreds of articles that run the gamut from the hardest of hard news stories – fires, kidnappings, politics – to the most narrative of non-fiction features: travel stories, essays, columns, and profiles. Her work has appeared largely in business-to-business magazines and daily newspapers, including The Boston Globe (she wrote for the paper weekly for more than 10 years and is still a regular contributor), and The Patriot Ledger – where she was a regular contributor with a beat for several years. She currently writes the occasional restaurant review for The Boston Globe, and wrote a food column for Boston.com for several years, entitled *The Dish*. She's ghost-written books, written book proposals that sold to mainstream publishers, and has authored and edited many other types of pieces: grants, press releases, corporate newsletters, website copy, blog posts, short histories for reference books, narrative biographies, and one (!) TV script, entitled Sex, (no) Drugs, & Rock 'n' Roll. To see Joan's newest website, please visit HelpForWomenWithADHD.com. Her food writing is compiled at GlobeSouthDish. com and you can find Joan on Instagram at HelpForWomenWithADHD.